When Jew and Christian Meet

When
JEW and CHRISTIAN
Meet

by LaVonne Althouse

With an Afterword by
RABBI BALFOUR BRICKNER
and DR. DAVID R. HUNTER

FRIENDSHIP PRESS NEW YORK

LIBRARY OF CONGRESS CATALOG CARD NUMBER: 66-11136

To Mother and Dad

Contents

The present search for understanding

ESPECIALLY FOR LEADERS

It is a privilege to be alive in the middle 1960's. Today all of mankind lives in a world where, although forces of divisiveness are vigorously at work breeding hostility and misunderstanding, there are also forces that seek to unify men by encouraging them to talk together and come to mutual understandings wherever possible.

Our world is controlled by neither demonic forces nor indifferent computers. We live, rather, in a world to which God the Creator is related and in which he calls his people to live in relationships of love to him and to all men and women. God the Redeemer makes it possible, by his power, for us to *try* to live in relationships of love to him and to each other.

Remembering all this, we need to look again at the history of Jewish-Christian relations. The encounter between Jews and Christians during the past two thousand

9

years has been marked by a profound ambivalence. On the one hand, Christians have taught love for the people to whom we are indebted for our Lord and faith and roots. On the other hand, we have often shown a contempt for this people, which has encouraged persecution of them and has caused unbelievable as well as unjustifiable suffering.

Some Evils of Anti-Semitism

In Chapter 3 we will discuss all too briefly the history of the Jewish people. For now let us consider what has been happening to them recently—during the past century and a half. Some of us in North America still do not realize that as recently as 1800 nearly all Jews in Europe were separated from the Christian populations, compelled to live in certain sections of cities called ghettos, and denied citizenship rights. During the eighteenth century, in the period known as the Enlightenment, a change came in Western Europe. Jews began to be considered citizens provided they declared allegiance to the countries in which they were living and regarded themselves as Jews only by reason of their religious loyalty. Where Jews were granted citizenship, they made significant contributions to the national government, culture, education, and general welfare.

Even as citizens, Jews endured periodic revivals of anti-Semitism. The persecution they experienced, unpredictably and unexpectedly, came to general attention only when it was especially flagrant. Let us look at two dramatic examples of recent anti-Semitism.

When in 1894, Captain Alfred Dreyfus, a French Jewish army officer, was falsely court-martialed for selling military secrets to Germany, anti-Semites pointed to his case as an example of evil arising from Semitic influence in government. Five years later someone else confessed to being responsible for the security breach, but twelve years passed before the Supreme Court of France exonerated Dreyfus. In this case anti-Semitism was used by monarchists and royalists to discredit republican government. A Jew became a convenient scapegoat.

Whether one man or millions of people are used for scapegoating, the practice is inhuman and wrong. Yet the injustice of the Dreyfus incident, which itself staggers the imagination, was to be repeated against millions of innocent people living in continental Europe under the Nazi regime.

A summary of Nazi practices indicates the depths that anti-Semitism can reach. Jews, who in Germany made up less than one percent of the population, were accused of socialist and communist tendencies (a false charge) and of exerting disproportionate influence in culture and education (a compliment to ability). On April 1, 1933, a nationwide boycott of Jews was ordered: Brown Shirts barricaded Jewish stores and Jewish-looking persons were beaten in the streets. By the Nuremburg Laws of September, 1935, intermarriage with Aryans became a crime punishable by death, Jews were disenfranchised, their young people were deprived of educational opportunities, famous Jewish scholars were dismissed, and publications of Jewish authors were banned.

11

This statue of Anne Frank stands in Utrecht, Netherlands, in memory of the Jews who were killed under the Nazi regime.

The murder of a minor official in the German Embassy at Paris, in 1938, was used as a pretext for a well-organized program of wrecking synagogues, stores, and homes. In addition, innumerable Jews were killed, thousands were sent to concentration camps, a fine of four hundred million dollars was imposed on the Jews, and movements of all Jews were restricted.

As the Nazis occupied countries of Central Europe, the persecution of Jews was extended. Jews from all occupied countries were forced to labor in the Krupp armament works; postwar investigations document brutality, starvation, and inhuman living conditions. Stories of six million Jews—one-third of the world Jewish population —slain in concentration camps are well documented, as are the reports of torture and bestial treatment they received in the camps.

The main reason for remembering these crimes is that they show us how inhuman people can become when they regard other people as less than human. The great misfortune is that these events are a part of, and arise out of, a general rejection of Jews simply because they are Jewish.

This rejection is often expressed in the creation of negative stereotypes of Jewish character that are believed without question: they are money-hungry, deceitful, aggressive, clannish, power-hungry, and subversive. When investigated, these charges prove to be nonsense for Jews as often as they are untrue for members of any other religion. But one characteristic, or even several, may be believed without question, and on the basis of

13

some unproved charge, Jews may be excluded from neighborhoods, jobs, and educational opportunities.

Behind all these false charges lurks the real reason for rejection: Jews are looked upon as those who crucified Jesus Christ. This is inaccurate—only Romans could condemn to death by crucifixion and execute the sentence. But, even more important than the inaccuracy of the charge, it has often caused us to forget that our Lord and his disciples were Jews. In rejecting all Jews for the role a few members of the priestly class may have had in seeking his death, we also reject our Lord and his disciples.

Recently Protestants have shown general concern that the teaching in church schools present an accurate picture of Jewish practices and Jewish-Christian relations. Dr. Bernhard Olson examined four sets of curriculum materials to determine what kinds of prejudice might be taught unconsciously through each of the courses. The results of the study are recommended to anyone interested in education, particularly Christian education. The information from the study had the salutary effect of helping curriculum planners recognize what was happening in the courses of study. Important corrections were made in curricula, which improved the effect of the materials on students' attitudes.

The study will be equally helpful to Christian education committees and all teachers in church or school. Anyone planning to teach may also be interested in studying these findings to see how one may unwittingly instill prejudice.

Some Steps Toward Overcoming Anti-Semitism

Not all Christians, however, have been unaware of the way prejudice becomes a part of the education we offer and the attitudes we teach. Many have been conscious of the insidiousness of prejudice and have spoken out against its dangers.

Some Christians also seek relationships with Jews. Dialogue is one kind of possible relationship. It has usually been conceived as an opportunity to increase respect, acceptance, and understanding between Christians and Jews so that they may work together on the problems of society, using the resources of both faiths to make the world a better place in which to live.

Another Christian approach to the Jew is widely known as the "parish approach," a missionary method significantly different from dialogue. Congregations are prepared to witness to Jews in their neighborhoods or places of work—wherever they frequently meet Jews. Sermons and education programs for adults and young people attempt to "train them to be Christian"—teach them how to demonstrate new life in Christ as love, compassion, and concern in order to win converts. Participants work to create goodwill toward the church, develop friendships with Jews, bring them to church, and invite them to become church members when they show a readiness.

This "parish approach" is rejected by Jews, as is any suggestion that Christianity is the one true faith to which they should be converted. Furthermore, Jews

Christian and Jewish young people meet to plan a dialogue.

New understandings of other persons and faiths can result.

sometimes misunderstand Christian intentions, frequently seeing in Christian friendliness a thinly veiled attempt to win them to Christianity.

Christians will say that they are not asked to force others to accept their faith, that conversion is the work of the Holy Spirit. They are, however, required to reveal the good news that they have been given and offer it to others. To this the Jew will respond in this spirit: You see, you cannot really enter into dialogue. You really want to convert us.

Through discussions in several conferences bearing the title, "The Church and the Jewish People," Christians and Jews have sought a basis for getting to know each other better. Such acquaintance and relationships of mutual trust, which can follow, are needed to prevent estrangement, persecution, and the attempt to destroy a whole people.

After the first conference on "The Church and the Jewish People" sponsored by the World Council of Churches in the early 1950's, a book was published containing the papers presented and discussed by Jewish and Christian theologians. In an introduction, Bishop Stephen Neill stated some essentials for helpful Jewish-Christian relationships. They may be summarized from his own words:

It is essential that Christian Churches and individual Christians interested in fellowship with Jews repudiate once for all, and from the heart, every method [of witnessing to their own faith] which in the light of the Gospel and of the human conscience must be condemned.

18

. . . The Jew too has to be asked to consider again his attitude to the witness of those of other faiths than his own.

There has been a tendency for Jews to condemn every Jew who has ever become a Christian. . . . This attitude must be wholly given up. . . .

Conversely, it must be recognized that the Jews have every right to bear witness to their faith and try to win others for it.

Of the sincere Christian it is demanded by his faith that in relation to the Jews he should not consider that his duty has been fulfilled by the exercise of tolerance and fair-mindedness. It is required of him that he desire understanding, deep sympathy, and even affection for the people of Israel.

Finally, the Christian is called to exercise towards the Jewish people, and towards those Jews whom he may happen to meet, the love which the Saviour showed and shows them.[1]

The Division of World Mission and Evangelism of the World Council of Churches has a committee concerned with Jewish-Christian relations. In 1959, together with what was then the National Council of Churches' Department of Evangelism, they began "A Biblical and Theological Study of the Church and Judaism," which still continues in many denominations in the United States and Canada. The ferment of concern that this study generated was directly responsible for the National Council's "Resolution on Jewish-Christian Relations," in 1964, which said in part:

[1] Notes may be found on page 91.

19

The spiritual heritage of Jews and Christians should draw us to each other in obedience to the one Father and in continuing dialogue; the historic schism in our relations carries with it the need for constant vigilance lest dialogue deteriorate into conflict. . . .

The General Board urges that the members of its constituent communions seek that true dialogue with the religious bodies of the Jewish community through which differences in faith can be explored within the mutual life of the one family of God—separated, but seeking from God the gift of renewed unity—knowing that in the meantime God can help us to find our God-given unity in the common service of human need.

A 1964 Lutheran consultation on "The Church and the Jewish People" was also a symposium of Christian and Jewish opinion on the intricate problem of relationships. Its findings spoke both of mission and of dialogue:

As a member of the body of Christ, every Christian also shares in the "sent-ness" of the church. This quality of "being sent" applies in every area of the Christian's relationship to the world, and he will witness with his whole life: in testifying to his faith, in listening to others, in seeking to understand, and in sharing the burdens of his fellowmen.

The witness to the Jewish people is inherent in the content of the gospel . . . [it] will most effectively reflect the glory of Christ . . . when it is pursued in the normal activity of the Christian congregation. . . .

It is a Christian responsibility to seek respectfully to understand both the Jewish people and their faith. Therefore responsible conversations between Christians and Jews are to be desired and welcomed.[2]

20

Here both witness and dialogue are named as acceptable positive means, from a Christian point of view, for seeking relationships with Jews. Among many Jews there is interest in dialogue with Christians, though they reject efforts to convert them to Christian faith.

This book is designed to prepare Christian teen-agers to meet Jews of their age group in dialogue. It will discuss reasons why they might enter dialogue, will supply background information and additional sources of help, and will suggest a program of preparation for dialogue. Although suggestions for dialogue subjects will be given and some guidelines about procedure will be offered, each group will be encouraged to choose its own areas of concern and prepare its own programs. By following the rules for dialogue listed in Chapter 1 and the guidelines for a dialogue program in Chapter 5, and by developing subjects out of the needs the group expresses, each dialogue in each community can develop into a discussion that is relevant and fruitful.

When Jew and Christian Meet

Christians who enter into dialogue with Jews see in it a new way of being obedient to their Lord. For dialogue is a commitment to talk openly and to listen willingly to the other person's beliefs. We listen because we respect the other as a responsible person with the right to believe and think and act freely so long as he remains responsible to his commitment to sincere dialogue.

Dialogue means facing up to the fact that we some-

21

times disagree in beliefs. For the Christian this conflict, of itself, does not alter his faith or affect his obedience to his Lord. It simply means that everyone remains open to new insights, which the Christian believes come from Jesus Christ, at every level of conversation and joint action.

Perhaps such dialogue could result in the true, deep sharing of faith between Christian and Jew in which both find more of God's will for their respective communities. Since, as was said previously, dialogue includes working together for practical social improvement, it offers opportunity to express concretely some of the meaning of redemption for this world and for all the people in it.

Those who enter into dialogue with Jews must realize that Jews are committed to live as one people until God's Messiah ends time and brings in the new age. The German Lutheran theologian Gunther Harder has made two points worth noting by those who engage in Jewish-Christian dialogue.

First, Harder points out, "The partner in Christian-Jewish conversation, the Jew who says No to Christ, is for the Christian . . . a living witness that God's power and grace are not at our disposal."[3] In other words, witness is the work of the believer; conversion is in the hands of God. The believer must both witness to the power of faith for his life and allow the witness to bear fruit as God wills.

Second, Harder finds that, in a world where Christ's lordship is still hidden, where he has not yet brought in his kingdom in its fullness, ". . . perhaps today, and in no small number of instances, it will be the task of the Christian to call the Jew to be really a Jew, and to remain a Jew, and thus to stand in the place where God's wisdom and patience has placed him."[4]

In short, we approach the Jew as the neighbor whom Jesus Christ has called us to know in the deepest sense and to love as our Lord loves us. From here we follow our own good sense and do as we please, so long as we desire and pray to be held fast by the love of Jesus Christ. Moreover, we offer up to God the dialogue we have with Jewish neighbors for his blessing, to bear fruit in his time as he ordains.

CHAPTER 1

Why talk things over?

AN INVITATION TO DIALOGUE

"Hi, Sara. You ready? Oh, excuse me, Rod, I didn't mean to interrupt." Mark Bronstein had seen Sara Goldman as he stepped on stage, but a piece of the scenery had hidden Rod Carter, and any particular voice was drowned in the general bustle as the cast and crew cleaned up to go home.

"That's all right, Mark. I'm leaving now to pick up Ellie, anyway. Guess orchestra practice must be over if you're here."

"Just got out. She's waiting for you, too; I saw her. How are the stars of the spring play doing today?"

"Oh, we're going to snow 'em next week, aren't we, Sara?" said Rodney, grinning. Then, a little more seriously: "No kidding, Mark, Sara's OK. Just wait till you hear her do the bluebird song."

Mark's hands went up in mock horror. "I have, I have! But say, Rod, why don't you pick up Ellie and meet us out back, and I'll drop you both. Dad let me have the car tonight."

"Great! See you in a couple of minutes."

The four met at the Bronstein family car minutes later and decided it was early enough for them to stop for sodas before going home. As they sat in the drugstore booth sipping their drinks, the conversation quickly turned to the play.

"I hope you won't let Becky Carson and Jim Parks hear you calling Sara and me the stars of the spring play, Mark," teased Rod. "Since they lead the second cast, I'll bet they think they're as good as we are!"

"I'm sure Becky'll do all right, but to me Sara's the real star," Mark replied loyally, with a smile at Sara. She blushed a little, but looked pleased.

"One thing puzzles me, though," said Ellie. "Since you two are in the first cast and are giving two of the three performances, why didn't you get to play on Friday night? That's sure to draw the biggest audience."

Sara dropped her eyes and seemed to catch her breath. "I didn't mean to make Rod miss anything big, Ellie. But I'm the cause of it. It was just that. . . ."

Rod interrupted. "Sara, for Pete's sake, if I'd wanted to play on Friday night, I could've asked to switch casts. Besides, Mr. Morrison made the decision about what nights each cast would play."

"Yes, Rod, but you know he put us on Wednesday and Thursday because I said I'd like to be with my family Friday night. You see, Ellie, Friday night for us is—well, it's something like Sunday is for you."

25

"Look, Sara, it's all right. Why, now I can take Ellie to the play Friday. We can be together, instead of her sitting there with her parents."

Ellie added earnestly, "I'm sorry, Sara. Guess I should have known. And I *would* rather see the play with Rod on Friday."

They all smiled, and the conversation continued as the boys paid for the sodas and the four climbed into the car to go home. When they got to Ellie's house, Rod, who lived next door, got out with Ellie.

"Thanks for the lift, Mark. It's much better than taking a bus," he said. "See you both tomorrow."

"See you tomorrow," they echoed as Mark drove on.

As Rod and Ellie walked toward Ellie's house, she said seriously, "Gosh, I hope I didn't hurt Sara. I should have known better, shouldn't I?"

"Maybe I should've told you," said Rod comfortingly. "But, honestly, Ellie, I never thought about it. It really isn't important, is it . . . to play on Friday night?"

"No, I guess not. Just one of those things a person says. I mean, Sara does have something more important to do. You know, Rod—maybe it would be good to know something about Jews—and what they believe, and all that."

"You mean, so you wouldn't put your foot in it when you talk to them?" Rod grinned.

"Oh, no—well, yes, maybe for that reason, too. But I mean, I wonder what they do on Friday night . . . and why. But I just can't walk up to Sara and ask her, 'What do you believe, Sara?' can I?"

26

Rod shook his head slowly, "No, Ellie. People don't do things like that."

Invitation to a Dialogue

This book is an invitation to meet new friends—or to meet some you already know in a new way. It suggests that your youth fellowship or other organization might enjoy and profit from a programmed effort to learn to know young people of another faith—the Jewish faith.

We will call this programmed effort a dialogue, although more than two people will take part. The dialogue will offer an opportunity for approximately equal numbers of Christian and Jewish young people to discuss what they believe and what their faith means in their daily lives. The discussions—the dialogue sessions—will be planned to help each person examine his own tradition and learn about another's faith.

Dialogue can help establish understanding between faiths in two important ways. First, it can help clear up false or distorted images, which Christians sometimes have of Jews and Jews sometimes have of Christians. Second, it may show that Jew and Christian have much to give and to receive from each other.

Dialogue between Christians and Jews is needed because even when members of the two faiths live near each other and work or attend school together, they often do not know each other. We tend to keep apart along faith lines, as we also often separate along racial, economic, or social lines. When we keep apart from each other, it is easy to get the wrong ideas about each other.

27

The Harm of Stereotypes

We call some inaccurate ideas stereotypes. Often we suppose stereotypes to be a kind of shorthand thinking. In fact, they represent no thinking at all, but result from uncritical acceptance of a general idea. They are oversimplified concepts that can rob us of true understanding and can sour human relations.

In an article called, "Don't Let Stereotypes Warp Your Judgment," Robert L. Heilbroner reported that:

A number of Columbia and Barnard [college] students were shown 30 photographs of pretty but unidentified girls, and asked to rate each in terms of "general liking," "intelligence," "beauty" and so on. Two months later, the same group were shown the same photographs, this time with fictitious Irish, Italian, Jewish and "American" names attached to the pictures. Right away the ratings changed. Faces which were now seen as representing a national group went down in looks and still farther down in likability, while the "American" girls suddenly looked decidedly prettier and nicer.[1]

This experiment showed some of the harm due to stereotyping. Indirectly it shows how we not only put people into categories, but how we show a preference for some categories over others. "American" girls were prettier and nicer—was this because we unconsciously thought they seemed more "like us"?

Usually we quickly carry this preference-by-stereotype much further. We may choose friends or even class officers unconsciously on this basis. Yet someone from "another group" may have a great deal to offer us as a friend or do a good, even superior, job as a class officer. But we have not chosen for quality; we have chosen by means of unconscious identification. We can make many kinds of wrong choices this way.

To check your own choice by identification, test yourself honestly on the story at the beginning of this chapter. The names chosen suggest something about the characters, don't they? Did you like any of them better than any others—immediately? What color hair and eyes does each boy or girl have? What kind of home does each live in? Are you thinking in terms of stereotypes as you answer these questions?

Heilbroner writes that

. . . we tend to stereotype because this helps us make sense out of a highly confusing world, a world which William James once described as "one great, blooming buzzing confusion." It is a curious fact that if we don't *know* what we're looking at, we are often quite literally unable to *see* what we're looking at. People who recover their sight after a lifetime of blindness actually cannot at first tell a triangle from a square.[2]

This writer admits that stereotypes are one way we define the world in order to see it and deal with it. But he also reminds us that stereotypes make us lazy. Worse yet, they get in the way of good judgment; so they may cause us to be unjust or unfair to others. Also, they may cause us to deprive ourselves of rewarding relationships. Stereotypes that Christians often believe to be characteristic of Jews are harmful in these ways.

29

How Dialogue Helps

When Christians and Jews decide to enter into dialogue, they may discover that they can deepen each other's insights into faith. The Old Testament is a common heritage, even though each faith interprets it somewhat differently. As we learn the other's interpretations and understandings, we shed new light on our own beliefs.

In dialogue we learn to trade stereotyped ideas about a group of people for facts about individuals. We take the time to get to know each other across group lines. We help ourselves develop the habit of listening to others and accepting them as they are rather than forming ideas about them based on notions we have heard from uninformed sources.

In dialogue we also come to see that others care about some of the problems we are concerned about. We discover we can join forces to correct things that are wrong or to accomplish something that needs to be done.

Finally, in dialogue, as we get to know each other, we may discover that God reveals to us something about himself and his will for our lives. Christians imbued with a "go and tell" attitude about their faith may miss a "come and see" call from their Lord if they enter every relationship intending to convince the other of the rightness of Christianity. In dialogue we plan to listen to the other and then tell about our own "good news" as the other inquires about our faith. This telling is a sharing of understanding, not an attempt to convert the other.

As we talk together we may hear God speaking to us through the other even though we disagree on some points. In any case, we are engaged in dialogue to learn by sharing and listening.

The Rules of Dialogue

Dialogue is a serious undertaking. It is an opportunity to speak together about the deepest areas of life, and these are very sensitive areas. Everyone must care about the other's feelings and must listen carefully to what the other is saying. No one should participate in dialogue who is not ready to keep the rules listed below.

These six rules have been taken from a chapter by the Reverend Robert McAfee Brown, in the book *An American Dialogue*.[3] Originally designed for Protestant-Catholic dialogue, they have been slightly revised to apply to Jewish-Christian relationships:

1. Each partner must believe that the other is speaking in good faith. This is the indispensable minimum for any kind of dialogue. As long as the Protestant feels that the Jew is simply trying to monopolize the conversation, he will be understandably reluctant to speak openly. As long as the Jew feels the Protestant is really out to convert him by catching him off guard in a weak moment, he will preclude the possibility of any good emerging from the discussion. Any dialogue must assume a common devotion to truth.

2. Each partner must have a clear understanding of his own faith, an eagerness to articulate his position, and

a real willingness to have it scrutinized in discussion.

3. Each partner must strive for a clear understanding of the faith of the other. This is both a precondition of dialogue and a result of it. There are plenty of misunderstandings that can be dissipated by a little honest reading. However, reading alone will never give a really clear understanding of the faith of the other. This can only come as a result of dialogue. For it will only be in some kind of give-and-take, face-to-face encounter that the most deep seated misunderstandings will be cleared up.

There are two important corollaries to this mutual striving for a clear understanding of the other:

a) The first of these is a willingness to interpret the faith of the other in its best light rather than its worst. This does not mean glossing over problems or pretending that grievous sins were never committed. It does mean that the best becomes our norm rather than the worst.

b) A second corollary follows from the attempt to get a clear understanding of the faith of the other. Each partner must maintain a continual willingness to revise his understanding of the faith of the other.

Dialogue can be a dangerous pastime, for it may force us to give up some of our most cherished caricatures, and these die hard.

4. Each partner must accept responsibility in humility and penitence for what his group has done and is doing to foster and perpetuate unnecessary divisions.

5. Each partner must forthrightly face the issues that cause separation as well as those that create unity. If certain disputants simply want to stress the differences between Judaism and Protestantism, there are others who in the name of a false kind of charity are unwilling to face the differences lest the atmosphere be soiled. Either avenue leads to the destruction of dialogue; the first because cynicism deepens separation, and the second because sentimentality paves the way for disappointment. It is far better for each partner to recognize at the start that no amount of emphasis upon points held in common will dissipate the differences that will remain. The differences ought to be recognized directly and forthrightly and openly, so long as they are not the only facts recognized. If they are stressed first, they may provide psychological deterrents to the initiation of the dialogue.

6. Each partner must recognize that all we can do with the dialogue is to offer it up to God. What "happens" as a result of the dialogue must be left strictly in his hands. If something is to issue from it, he will see to it that something does. If we attempt to manipulate the dialogue, or "use" it, we may be sure that we will thwart whatever potential good lies in it. If, in typical North American fashion, we are immediately impatient for "results," we will simply have to learn something about the patience of God or we will try his patience still further. We must not, in other words, participate in the dialogue with our preconceived notions as to precisely where it should lead.

Conclusion

In these pages we have described the reasons you are invited into dialogue with Jewish young people and the rules by which dialogue must operate. Before setting out, however, you will want to know something about Jews and the history of Jewish-Christian relations. Then you may wish to prepare for dialogue by a series of programs suggested in Chapter 5. After that, beyond some suggestions for beginning dialogue, you are on your own!

CHAPTER 2

Israel, God's chosen

SOME QUESTIONS AND ANSWERS

A young man was lamenting that just when he was ready to declare that he had gotten Judaism "completely out of his system," Friday night came along, and he had the feeling that he ought to be having dinner with his family, and he knew that he would always be a Jew.[1]

Who Is a Jew?

Who is a Jew? That is a complex question. Although it is usually related to birth, it is also, above all, a matter of faith and practice.

Any baby born of a Jewish mother is a Jew. The mother is responsible for keeping the home "religious" and has a key role in many home rituals. The father, as head of the household, sees that the children are educated and brought up in the fear of God. Close family ties, significant family responsibilities, and the close relationship of many festivals to family living all help to make Jewish

35

identity at least partly a matter of family relationship. In the kosher home all members of the family have some interest in homemaking because of its religious significance.

Jews are not a race. Jewish believers include members of all races, Negro, Oriental, and Caucasian. In this respect they are no different from Christian believers, the faithful of the Muslim world, or the followers of any other world-circling faith.

The adult Jew is, however, distinctively something more than just a child of certain parents. A Jew is one who believes he is a member of a people chosen by God at Mt. Sinai to show other peoples how God wishes his children to live on earth. The precise meaning of this belief has been reinterpreted generation by generation, but essentially Jews understand they are chosen for a task—to proclaim *how* God is Lord.

At the age of thirteen the Jewish son or daughter assumes personally the religious responsibility of an adult, which is obedience to the commandments of God. For boys this is the *bar mitzvah*; the ritual for girls is called *bas mitzvah*. The commandments are contained in the Torah, which has been called "the embodiment of the word of God, the expression of the Divine Will for mankind. . . . Every Jew who lives by the Torah is a person whose life is an expression of the love of God and of his fellow-men."[2]

Among some Jews only boys covenant publicly to assume responsibility for their acts as sons of the covenant; among others, both boys and girls promise faithfulness before the assembled congregation. A person remains a

A Jewish boy holds a Torah as he stands ready to assume personal religious responsibility at his bar mitzvah.

Jew for life unless he or she rejects the faith by a public declaration and adopts another.

Jews believe the Torah is a divinely inspired discipline that enables man to know truth and to practice mercy, love, and justice. The man or woman who does justice and loves mercy and kindliness shows that he or she has accepted the kingship of God. For this reason, the moral deed is of utmost importance. The observance of rituals is important as a discipline in accepting the will of God.

Life for the Jew is the holiest value, for God created it and the world, and he gave the world to man to keep and preserve. It is good. "Wherefore a man should treasure it, not despise it; affirm and not deny it; have faith in it and never despair of its possibilities. For behind it is God."[3] The enhancement of life— the quest to engender, preserve, and perfect it—is called by Rabbi Ben Zion Bokser a "Second Scripture," and the ethical deed is "the deed which furthers the unfolding life of the universe" and "shows respect for God's purpose in creation."[4]

How Does Judaism Differ from Christianity?

At this point one may ask, "What is the difference between Judaism and Christianity if all these things are true about Judaism?" Detailed differences would require much more space to describe than is available here, but two key differences may be identified that may be helpful.

Jews, for example, find difficulty with the Christian's belief in the triune God. Their belief is summed up in the Shema: "Hear, O Israel: The Lord our God is one Lord." One and not two, they insist; one and not three.

Christians, too, believe in one God, but with a difference. They would say as, for instance, Huldreich Zwingli:

First of all, I both believe and know that God is one and He alone is God, and that He is by nature good, true, powerful, just, wise, the Creator and Preserver of all things, visible and invisible; that Father, Son and Holy Spirit are indeed three persons, but that their essence is one and single.[5]

The idea that God is one substance, yet three persons, is basic to Christian faith. Another basic belief is that the Word, by whom the world was created, became human flesh, was born at a certain time in history, and became the world's Redeemer.

Analogies have been used to explain how these beliefs can be true logically, but they always seem to break down at some point. Yet fifteen hundred years after the Councils of Nicea and Chalcedon, where acceptable affirmations of these beliefs were adopted, Christians continue to seek ways to explain them to non-Christians. Anyone who enters into dialogue will likely have to put into words his own understanding of the Trinity and the Incarnation at some time or another.

Another question to which members of the two faiths give quite different answers is: "What are you doing here?"

Jews believe their faith is one of many ways to God, all of which are important and significant. They believe that Jews have a mission from God to bear witness to his truth by word and deed—by obeying the Torah. In so doing, they try to be an example of the way God wants all people to live together harmoniously. As the Union Prayerbook, used by all Reform congregations in North America, says:

Almighty and merciful God, Thou has called Israel to Thy service and found him worthy to bear witness to Thy truth among the peoples of the earth. Give us grace to fulfil this mission with zeal tempered by wisdom and guided by regard for other men's faith. May our life prove the strength of our own belief in the truths we proclaim. May our bearing toward our neighbors, our faithfulness in every sphere of duty, our compassion for the suffering and our patience under trial show that He whose law we obey is indeed the God of all goodness, the Father of all men. . . .[6]

Christians see the role of the faithful community quite differently. Two verses from the New Testament sum up their understanding:

But you are a chosen race, a royal priesthood, a holy nation, God's own people, that you may declare the wonderful deeds of him who called you out of darkness into his marvelous light. (1 Peter 2:9)

Go therefore and make disciples of all nations, baptizing them in the name of the Father and of the Son and of the Holy Spirit, teaching them to observe all that I have commanded you; and lo, I am with you. . . .
(Matthew 28:19, 20)

By these verses we see that Christians are called to do something different from setting examples, though setting examples may be one way of fulfilling their task. They are told to invite all people to share their fellowship and

40

way of life, and so to share redemption through Jesus Christ. In their belief, the "chosen people" are not called to set examples for others, but to become part of the new creation God has established in his world and to share this new life with all others.

Where Do Jews Live Today?

The Jewish faith, like our own, includes people of every race on every settled continent. Today they number more than 13 million people.

About half of these Jews live in North America. Almost 6 million live in the United States; about 250,000 in Canada.

In Latin America Jews number about 750,000.

Nearly 3 million Jews live in the Soviet Union and its Eastern European satellite countries. Over a million more live in Western Europe; of these 450,000 are in Great Britain, 500,000 in France, and about 250,000 in the remaining countries.

In Israel the Jewish population is about 2 million; in the rest of Asia there are about 122,000 Jews.

In Africa there are about 285,000 Jews, mainly in Morocco, Algeria, Tunisia, and the Union of South Africa.

All Jews born or naturalized in any country are citizens of that country. In North America, where they live and work with people of other faiths, they are Americans of Jewish faith, even as Roman Catholics and Protestants are considered Americans of their own respective faiths. It is true that in ancient times Israel was a separate nation in the Middle East with its own king and homeland. Before Romans destroyed the second temple in A.D. 70, they were a nation among other nations.

After the temple was destroyed, Jews began to think of themselves as essentially a religious community. But this religion continued to be identified with a certain people who had been a nation and were now exiled from a homeland. During the Middle Ages, when Jews in Western Europe were persecuted and made to live in ghettos, they continued to think of themselves as a separate people in exile.

At the beginning of the nineteenth century under Napoleon, for the first time in hundreds of years, Jews of Western Europe were permitted to become part of the political, civic, economic, and social life of the communities and nations where they lived. This came about as a new idea of nationalism taught that any person, whatever his race or religion, could become a citizen of the nation in which he was born or lived and to which he pledged his undivided allegiance. In countries where Jews could become a part of the community, many began to emphasize the religious aspects of their Jewishness and to minimize the idea of exile. Though minimized it was never forgotten.

In Russia and Eastern Europe, for example, where national rights were not granted, the Jewish community continued to emphasize the idea of exile and to nourish the hope for return to Zion.

Since 1948 there has again been a nation in the world called Israel. Any Jew from any country in the world may go to live in it. North American Jews show concern for Israel and extend help to the people. But essentially they consider themselves American and Canadian citizens who practice the Jewish faith.

Why Are There Different Kinds of Jews?

In North America there are three major groupings in Judaism called Orthodox, Reform, and Conservative Judaism. Reform Judaism arose in Western Europe as a result of the new nationalism that released Jews from ghettos and encouraged them to take their places in modern community life. Reform Judaism has tried to help Jews live in the spirit of the Torah as citizens of modern countries where institutions and values have become increasingly secularized. It has appealed to many who were leaving a faith that seemed irrelevant to daily life.

Orthodox Judaism continues to flourish in Eastern Europe. Nineteenth century immigrants from those countries brought it to North America. Many of their descendants still adhere to the ancient beliefs and practices it preserves, even as they contribute much to the arts, business, and professions in the mainstream of North American life.

Near the end of the nineteenth century in North America a group of Jews formed a third group of interpreters of Jewish faith. They found Reform Judaism lacking in something they considered important but sought an expression of Judaism other than orthodoxy. It is called Conservative Judaism. Conservative Jews seek a middle way between "modernists" and "traditionalists."

43

What Are Some Current Problems Facing Judaism?

After more has been said about faith and ritual, it will be possible to describe the more important differences between these three interpretations. For the moment it is enough to indicate that all three kinds of Judaism face challenges and questions from science, secularism, and changing value systems similiar to those faced by Christians. Young adults of both faiths struggle to find answers to questions such as: If man learns how to create life, will it be sacred as God-created life is sacred? Where is God? As man learns to control his environment more and more, will he usurp God's authority? How is God Lord of my life today?

Jews also have problems we do not share. In the first place being a minority people (6 million among 193 million in the United States), Jews have a very real fear of being assimilated and losing their identity as a people.

The opposite problem, the experience of anti-Semitism, is unfortunately a widespread and difficult one. Social rejection is perhaps the most prevalent form it takes in North America, although Jews may lose opportunities for jobs, housing, and education because of their faith.

As we enter into dialogue, we will learn more about these problems and try to understand them. Some difficulties, notably overcoming anti-Semitism, can be tackled together. Some problems, such as the challenges of a scientific, secular, industrial culture, can be shared sympathetically; insights can be gained from both sides as they are discussed.

CHAPTER 3

"You only have I known . . ."

A VERY BRIEF HISTORY

"You only have I known of all the families of the earth," said the prophet Amos on behalf of the Lord to the children of Israel. "Know" in this sense means "to have a deep personal relationship with someone," to know someone intimately.

Generations earlier, God was believed to have said to Abraham, "I will make of you a great nation, and I will bless you, . . . and by you all the families of the earth will bless themselves." (Genesis 12:2, 3) The story of God's call to Abraham is recorded against a background of "world history" as the Jewish people remembered and told it in Genesis—the particular history of God's dealings with men until he chose a people who would reveal his sovereignty over all men.

Some have suggested that God chose Israel because the people had a "genius for religion"; others have feared that such chosenness implies that these people believe

45

they are better than others. The story of Israel indicates something quite different from either of these ideas. Events from the call of Abraham to the redemption of Israel from slavery in Egypt testify again and again to the free choice of a loving God who has set a task for his people and who will not let them choose another, much worse, servitude.

When Israel covenanted to be God's people and keep his commandments at Sinai, therefore, she did so out of gratitude, not only for deliverance from slavery, but for God's all-encompassing love that would not let the people separate from him. The men and women who accepted the covenant could remember the slavery that resulted from dependence on an earthly power rather than on God. When they accepted the covenant to do God's commandments, they accepted a relationship in which their obedience would show their loving gratitude to God for giving them their land and for the supreme gift, life. In return they promised to obey God as required by the Torah— the laws and teachings that governed their community.

We need to understand that Israel loved the Torah because it helped establish her relationship to God, which was the only good and real life. Keeping the laws meant living in harmony with God's design of creation. Her whole history as a people with a land was recorded from the perspective of her obedience or disobedience which kept or broke her relationship with God.

While she lived in the land God gave her, Israel understood that she must keep the Torah to show her obedience. The entire verse of which we quoted a portion at the beginning of this chapter reads, "You only have I known of all the families of the earth; therefore I will punish you for all your iniquities." (Amos 3:2) Even if she disobeyed, Israel would be known as God's people by his chastisement.

The destruction of the kingdoms of Israel and Judah was interpreted by the prophets as punishment for disobedience. But as the people lived in exile, the prophets continued to assure Israel that God would not forget his people.

When the people finally won the right to rebuild the temple and some were allowed to return to Jerusalem, Ezra, a priest and scribe, reawakened in them an awareness of their responsibilities as Jews to love and keep the Torah. They covenanted to do this by living apart from other people in family and communal life. As with all such separations, some aspects of this decision met with protest from the community itself, as in the story of Ruth. In the end the separation party triumphed for a time.

A synagogue was built in the new temple so that the communal teaching of the essence of the Law to the young would continue as it had begun during the Babylonian exile. Teaching in synagogue and sacrifices in temple remained central to Judaism while the people lived together in their own land, whether they were free or conquered. In A.D. 70 the temple, including its synagogue, was destroyed and the people were again dispersed and deprived of their homeland. During this period the synagogues, as houses of prayer, of study, and of communal life, continued to keep Judaism alive and the Pharisees continued to interpret the Torah, Prophets, and Writings, the holy Scriptures of the dispersed Jewish people.

Judaism in the Christian Era

From 350 B.C. to A.D. 200 wise men and rabbis interpreted, explained, and amplified the meaning of Torah. The vast body of material, including laws, regulations for festivals and holy days, ethical and moral ideals, and spiritual values, was compiled and edited about A.D. 200 and became known as the Mishnah (teaching).

Succeeding generations found it necessary to reinterpret the Mishnah through commentary and explanation. This literature, covering the years from A.D. 200 to 500, was compiled as the Gemara (completion); it covers every aspect of Jewish belief, tradition, and all laws regulating man's relation to God and to his fellowman.

Mishnah and Gemara together make up the Talmud, a word derived from the Hebrew *lomed*, "to study." Two editions of the Gemara were compiled, one in Palestine and another in Babylonia. The latter is the more thorough and more generally authoritative on Judaism.

Study of this "veritable encyclopedia of Jewish literature touching all phases of life and thought" is a demanding task. Regulations relating to any particular situation are scattered through it and must be culled out, compared, and contemplated to determine their meaning for a new situation. Those who devote their lives to this task, vital to the religious community, have always been held in high esteem, and study of the Torah itself came to be regarded as an act of worship.

48

During the centuries when the Talmud was developing, some Jews followed the ancient Roman roads into the interior of Europe, where they settled and for a time lived peaceably. Others settled along North African trade routes and, with the Arabs, entered Spain. There they engaged in commerce, developed a literature, and made contributions to philosophy. For these Spanish Jews a Golden Age of learning came between the tenth and the thirteenth centuries.

The towering figure of this Golden Age was Moses Maimonides. Born in 1135, Maimonides came to maturity just as a revival of Aristotelean belief in reason was challenging Jewish and Christian faiths. "Using an Aristotelean framework, he taught the harmony of reason and revealed truths, declaring that revelation is necessary to supplement reason, but cannot be contrary to it. He explained the miracles rationally, interpreted much of the material in Genesis allegorically, and spoke of the anthropomorphic descriptions of God as figures of speech."[1] In short, his *Guide to the Perplexed* did for Judaism in his day something akin to what Aquinas' *Summa Theologica* did for twelfth century Christianity.

A reaction from those who feared that this rationalizing would reduce Judaism to a philosophy produced a body of mystical literature known as the Cabala, the tradition. These ideas were supposed to have been handed down by certain initiates, hidden from ordinary people, and incapable of transmission through ordinary rational channels. Cabala provided a counterbalance for a totally rationalistic understanding of Judaism, just as the ration-

49

al interpretation safeguarded the faith from the superstitious tendencies to which cabalism was susceptible.

The Golden Age produced great scientists, craftsmen, poets, philosophers, and theologians among the Jews who contributed to the economic, social, and cultural life of Western Europe. This age came to an end as the Crusades awakened in Christians a hatred not only of the infidel in the Holy Land, but also of the unbeliever in their own communities.

Spanish and Portuguese Jews, known as Sephardic Jews, were persecuted severely by the notorious Inquisition and finally expelled by King Ferdinand and Queen Isabella in 1492. They fled mostly to Holland and the New World. After the crusades Jews were not permitted to own land or to farm in Austria, Germany, and Italy. Their right to enter professions was severely restricted. For a time, they were forced to become money-lenders (really forerunners of modern bankers and the first to operate on international lines); then they were finally barred from this profession, too. Forced to live in ghettos and to wear "Jew badges" when they ventured into other parts of the city, they suffered torment and extreme poverty. They became "invisible" and were denied both the justice and the compassion their own faith commanded them to practice continually toward all others.

The synagogue, the Talmud with its pattern for living, and a common language among the northern European Jews or Ashkenazim, called Yiddish, bound the scattered communities of persecuted Jews tightly together. It also intensified the hope for the Messiah who would deliver them and take them to a land where they could live again as a free people.

The Enlightenment Brings Changes

The trials and tribulations of ghetto life were to come to an end, not through the work of the Messiah, but through a change of heart and mind resulting from a new period of rationalism, the eighteenth century Enlightenment. The same period that laid the foundation for the American and French Revolutions and saw the revival of humanism and the beginnings of modern democracy caused a reappraisal of attitudes toward Jews.

In 1806 this change of heart and mind became a political fact when Napoleon Bonaparte declared that all persons who would pledge undivided allegiance to France should have equal civil and political rights. Specifically, Jews who regarded themselves as Frenchmen, differing from their fellow citizens only in religion, were proclaimed free citizens. Jews refer to this admission to the modern European community as their Emancipation.

Although most settlers of North America had come from Europe, with its practices of discrimination against Jews, Jewish settlers found they were accorded the same religious liberty as their fellow colonists. Of course, attitudes varied from colony to colony. But the prosperous commercial seaports of Boston, Newport, New York, Philadelphia, and Charleston needed the services of able Jewish merchants, who were highly respected by their neighbors.

Napoleon's decree in Europe and the new freedom to

become a part of the larger community in America marked a new day for the Jewish faith. Again, adaptation and interpretation would be needed. Although the Napoleonic decree was revoked after Waterloo and a new period of persecution began, and although things would not always be well everywhere even in North America, a change had come. Judaism would again attempt to adapt to the change.

The first attempt to adjust arose in Europe and became known as Reform Judaism. Its exponents placed high emphasis upon reason and pleaded for the discarding of forms that seemed useless. In the late eighteenth century in Germany they founded a modern religious school, built a temple with an organ and arranged a ritual in which hymns, prayers, and sermons in the German language were added to those in Hebrew. The movement took hold after much opposition.

In Reform Judaism, religious life centers and builds on the spirit of the Law and the prophetic concepts rather than their letter. Belief in a personal Messiah who will restore the Davidic monarchy gives way to belief that the role of the Jewish people is to set an example in faith and action which will usher in the Messianic Age. Belief in the restoration of a national state in the traditional Jewish homeland is optional. Belief in a personal and collective immortality is seldom clearly defined. Both the language of the nation in which the Jews are living and the Hebrew language are used in worship services.

Orthodox Jews are far more traditional. For them the written and oral Law (Torah and Talmud) are divine truth. These are chiefly interpreted by means of the Shulhan Aruch, an authoritative code written in the sixteenth century by Joseph Karo of Poland. To this Moses Isserles later added extended glosses incorporating religious customs of Germany and of Poland, thus making the Shulhan Aruch authoritative for those countries and, ultimately, for all of Europe.

Orthodox Jews believe the Messiah will come to redeem his people and begin a reign of universal peace. He will lead his people back to Jerusalem, restore the temple and its sacrifices, and establish Israel as a nation. They may believe in both the immortality of the soul and the resurrection of the body.

Between these two interpretations, a third, moderately reforming or moderately traditional way had developed, known as Conservative Judaism. Rabbi Mordecai Waxman describes its spirit:

Conservative Judaism feels that the legal system of Judaism, its rituals and its observances, should be examined in the light of the needs and situation of the Jewish people. Whatever changes are necessary must be made in the Spirit of Jewish law and in evolutionary rather than revolutionary fashion.[2]

As these varieties of Judaism have sought to relate their traditions faithfully to life in the modern world, Jews have been exposed to varying degrees of acceptance and persecution. They have often been excluded by the remainder of the community. Exclusion causes estrangement and estrangement gives rise to false rumors of undesirable character traits and practices. When a victim is sought to explain some difficulty or misfortune, he may be sought among these people. Children, learning of the crucifixion story and being taught inaccurately the facts of the New Testament, sometimes torment and hurt Jewish classmates. The slurring references they hear adults make about Jewish neighbors only confirm their misguided conclusions and justify their hostile actions.

Some of the violent and inhuman consequences of anti-Semitism in recent history were discussed in the introduction. After that, especially in Chapter 1, we tried to see how such false concepts have arisen throughout history through stereotype thinking, and some of the injustice they produce in our society.

Recent history of the Jewish people covers more than just anti-Semitism and persecution. It is studded with the contributions of individuals to the communities in which they live and, for the Jew, it is highlighted by the re-emergence of a nation called Israel.

The modern state of Israel was born on May 14, 1948. Its territory includes 7,993 square miles of desert country and three major seaports. In addition to Jews living there when the country was formed, immigrant Jews have come from all over the world to establish homes there. Any Jew of any nation is welcome to settle in Israel.

American Jews have a variety of attitudes toward Israel. A few have gone to live there, although by far the majority of new Israeli citizens have come from Europe, Africa, the Near East. For the most part, ties of senti-

Young Israelis dance the "Hora," a traditional Palestinian dance, to celebrate the birthday of their nation, founded on May 14, 1948, as a home for Jews from around the world.

ment, religion, and philanthropy bind North American Jews to the people of Israel, while their allegiance remains firm to the countries and communities in which they live.

Contributions to Community Life

History is made by people. The recent history of Jews in North America can perhaps best be examined in terms of the many contributions members of this faith community have made to national and civic life.

If a devout Jew were asked to name the greatest contribution his people have made to the world, he would probably answer that it is belief in one God who is Lord of creation, or the example Jews are called to set before men showing how God wishes men to live. A less orthodox, more humanitarian Jew might feel that the calling to preserve and enhance life is of highest importance.

Certainly Jews have contributed all of these things. They have also donated their own abilities and talents in every area of social, economic, and political life in North America. Among well known Jews are physician Jonas Salk; scientist I. I. Rabi; Governor Herbert H. Lehman; violinists Mischa Elman, Jascha Heifetz, and Yehudi Menuhin; composers Jerome Kern, Irving Berlin, George Gershwin, and Ernest Bloch; playwrights Paddy Chayefsky and Arthur Miller; novelists Herman Wouk, Edna Ferber, and Norman Mailer; actors Paul Muni, Eddie Cantor, and Danny Kaye; labor leader Samuel Gompers; businessmen Henry Morgenthau, Sr., and Julius Rosenwald of Sears Roebuck.

Jews have played important roles in all walks of North American life. Jewish businessmen and bankers helped develop national economies at the same time that Jewish labor leaders were aiding in the development of a strong union movement to distribute wealth, increase the buying power of all segments of society, and so contribute to economic growth and prosperity. Jewish attorneys and jurists such as Brandeis, Cardoza, Frankfurter, and Goldberg and legislators such as Ribicoff, Javits, and Celler have worked for political justice and the securing of constitutional rights. Jewish social agencies open their services to all in the community who need them.

Study, particularly study of the Law, has always been highly valued in the Jewish community. Moreover, Jews frequently have had to excel in a field in order to advance at all. These factors have combined to produce outstanding Jewish scholars in the humanities and sciences.

Jewish creative and interpretative artists, impressarios, and wealthy patrons have contributed generously to North American cultural life. Millions have pondered works in the Guggenheim Art Museum or have listened attentively to orchestras conducted by Leonard Bernstein (sometimes playing his own music).

These contributions indicate the value of the Jew in the North American community. To Christians everywhere they have given something even more precious than their significant participation in society. For it was out of this community that our own Savior came; in the light of its faith-history his work must be interpreted.

CHAPTER 4

All of life is worship

RITUAL OBSERVANCES

"Here come Ruth and David," said Sue. The half-dozen fellows and girls in the hospital residence lounge turned toward the door to greet the newcomers.

"How was the weekend at home?" asked Mike.

"Oh, we made some more wedding plans," came the expected answer from Ruth, as she smiled and blushed slightly.

"Important plans," said David. "Ruth decided she's going to keep a kosher home!"

"Then we chose patterns for the two sets of dishes," reported Ruth. For a while she and David took turns describing the details of setting up a kosher household, for no one else in the group understood what that meant.

Even afterward its meaning was not clear to all. Sue was heard remarking to a friend, "I've never seen a man so interested in housekeeping as David—not in all my life. And he's going to be a professional man, a doctor!"

58

ALL OF LIFE IS WORSHIP

The Importance of the Jewish Home

The home is a vital center of Jewish religious life; the faith has been family-centered from its beginning. Members of the family each have obligations and responsibilities for serving the whole group. Holy days offer occasions for the gathering of the "extended family" (aunts, uncles, grandparents, in-laws, cousins) to celebrate their faith together through home rituals, use of foods with special significance, and even games and dancing.

The great German poet Heinrich Heine once remarked that the Jewish people had a "portable religion" that could be carried with them wherever they went. The vehicle of this portable religion is the Jewish home, the vital center of Jewish life . . . through many centuries of persecution and insecurity, . . . they maintained their religious life and values through family-centered ritual in the home.[1]

Entering Jewish homes, one can often see on the right doorpost a mezuzah, a small case enclosing a scroll on which is written: "Hear, O Israel: The Lord our God is one Lord; and you shall love the Lord your God with all your heart, and with all your soul, and with all your might." (Deuteronomy 6:4, 5) These and additional verses from the Shema, Deuteronomy 6:4-9, 11:13-20, are inscribed in Hebrew on the scroll in obedience to the command: "And you shall write [the commandments] on the doorposts of your house and on your gates." (Deuteronomy 6:9) The mezuzah will be found on the right doorpost of the entrance to every room.

Mothers in Orthodox, Conservative, and some Reform

59

homes keep the house kosher, which simply means "fit and proper." Certain foods, such as pork products and shellfish, are forbidden; those permitted must be prepared in a prescribed manner. A restriction against mixing meat and milk foods requires the use of two distinctively different sets of dishes and cooking utensils in preparing and serving meals.

The organization of home and of family life, the Sabbath observance, and the rituals of the Jewish year all bind this community of people together in the effort to worship God by enhancing life and so to fulfill the Law obediently, as God's sons and daughters are called to do.

Centrality of the Sabbath

The Sabbath (from *shabbos* or *shabbat,* "to rest"), the seventh day of the week, is set aside for rest, relaxation, contemplation, or study of the Law and, always, for worship of the God who commanded its observance. It is the only holy day mentioned in the Ten Commandments. No physical labor may be performed on the Sabbath.

Sabbath, like all Jewish festivals, begins and ends at sunset. Shortly before the hour when the Sabbath begins on Friday evening, the mother lights candles and prays, "Blessed art thou, O Lord our God, King of the universe, who has sanctified us with His commandments, and commanded us to kindle the Sabbath light." She may add a prayer for the members of the household. On the family's return from the synagogue, the father blesses the children and the wine and hallah, two twisted loaves of bread.

60

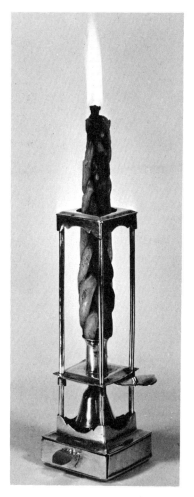

A Havdalah candle, lighted at sundown, shines on the departure of the Sabbath.

Wine, from a cup such as this silver goblet, extinguishes the candle at the end of the Sabbath.

שׁל כְּרִיּוּת

The family again attends service in the synagogue on Saturday morning. On Saturday evening the family gathers for a benediction said over wine and spices kept in a special box, whose fragrance soothes the soul from its distress at the leaving of the Sabbath. Following the blessing, a special braided candle is lit to shine on the departure of this "Queen of Days" who has been a welcome guest in the home. The candle is extinguished with wine and all wish each other a good week. This is Havdalah, "separation," and it separates the Sabbath from the rest of the week, as the kiddush, blessing, does at the beginning of Sabbath.

According to Jewish tradition, the Sabbath provides a foretaste of the days to come. In its joyful calm, people become aware of how beautiful the world may be. . . . Today, in a troubled and turbulent world, the Sabbath provides an opportunity for study, contemplation, and sociability, and for the peace through which people can realize that the earth of God's handiwork is good—as He judged it good.[2]

Other Important Festivals

"The annual cycle of religious holydays and festivals, the beautiful symbols and ceremonies in the Jew's daily life, are a recurring drama helping to renew and to revitalize for the Jews in every generation their Jewish ideals and traditions, their hopes and dreams for themselves and for mankind," writes Rabbi Levine.[3] In this chapter we can briefly illustrate the meaning of this statement by highlighting some of the more important Jewish festivals. Much more information is available in books indicated in the reading list.

ALL OF LIFE IS WORSHIP

Like Christians, Jews observe the beginning of their religious year at a different time from the January 1 beginning of the secular year. The Jewish equivalent of the First Sunday in Advent is Rosh Hashanah. Observed in September, it ushers in a season of self-examination, self-searching, repentance, and atonement. The shofar, a ram's horn, calls Jews to the synagogue for repentance, recalling the attempted sacrifice of Isaac by Abraham, and summons them to introspection, self-evaluation, and renewal of spiritual life.

At a festive dinner on Rosh Hashanah eve, the father recites the kiddush, a blessing over the holiday cup of wine, which is shared by each member of the family. Everyone also eats fruit dipped in honey, symbolizing hope for the coming year to be full of sweetness.

Morning prayers in the synagogue include one for the coming of universal brotherhood and peace. Reading the story of Abraham's willingness to sacrifice Isaac reminds all of the meaning of their commitment.

• **YOM KIPPUR**

Ten days after Rosh Hashanah comes another autumn holiday, Yom Kippur (the Day of Atonement), a time of fasting, prayer, and penitence. On this day Jews ask God for forgiveness and try to right wrongs committed toward their neighbors. On the evening it begins, in the beautiful Kol Nidre (prayer of all vows), the people ask forgiveness for breaking any vows made to God that they have not been able to fulfill. Those who tried but could not fulfill promises made to God can then be at peace once more with him and with their own consciences. The evening and following day are spent in prayer and worship in the synagogue. The Yizkor, a memorial service for the departed, recited four times during the year, also is recited on this day.

• **SUKKOTH**

Sukkoth, the festival of Booths, the first rite of the new year, commemorates temporary homes the Hebrews inhabited in the wilderness as they followed Moses to the promised land. Usually a sukkah or booth is built near the synagogue for the entire congregation. Walls are fragile; the roof would not protect dwellers from rain —in fact, it is left partly open so that a worshiper may look up at the stars and contemplate the heavens. This fragile sukkah reminds the worshiper that his sustenance and security depend "not upon material things which are, at best, transitory, but upon God, who is eternal."[4]

In the synagogue on Sukkoth, *lulav,* "green palm branches," *ethrog,* "yellow citrons," myrtle, and willow are waved in all directions at one point in the service to show that God, who is being thanked for his gifts of harvest, is found everywhere.

• **SIMHATH TORAH**

During the year, the entire first five books of Jewish Scripture are read section by section at synagogue services. On the ninth and last day of Sukkoth, Day of

Rejoicing over the Torah, the reading is completed. On Simhath Torah eve the reading of the closing chapter of Deuteronomy is preceded by a procession carrying the sacred scrolls around the synagogue. Children follow the procession merrily with banners and songs. The next morning a similar procession precedes the reading of the first chapter of Genesis. This holy day demonstrates that the study of God's word is an unending process.

• HANUKKAH

One of the two best known Jewish festivals, Hanukkah, the Festival of Dedication, falls in the month of December, in the Advent season. It commemorates the recapture of the temple (165 B.C.) in Jerusalem by Judah Maccabee after a Syrian-Greek emperor, Antiochus IV Epiphanes, had profaned it. For Jews this festival celebrates the fight for freedom to worship God.

Tradition relates that as the men cleansed the temple after routing the enemy, they found a single jar of holy oil, enough to keep the eternal light burning before the holy ark one day. They lighted it and it burned eight days. Judah Maccabee therefore proclaimed a period of eight holy days to rededicate the temple. This rededication is commemorated each year with gift giving, singing, and the lighting of the eight-candle menorah or candelabra. One candle is added each night until all are lighted on the last evening. Hanukkah, symbolizing the triumph of faith in God over earthly might, has often been a source of comfort and inspiration to those who struggle faithfully against overwhelming odds or enemies.

A candle is lighted on each of Hannukah's eight holy days.

• PASSOVER

After Hamishah Asar Bishvat, the new year of the trees, and Purim, which commemorates Queen Esther's faithfulness and the defeat of Haman of Persia, comes another well-known Jewish festival, Passover, a spring festival our Lord celebrated with his disciples. This high and holy festival season, which lasts for eight days, commemorates the deliverance of Israel from Egypt. Only unleavened bread is eaten during the period. On the first evening (first two evenings in Conservative and Orthodox homes) the family gathers to share the Seder, a ritual meal at which the story of the redemption is told, accompanied by songs, prayers, and blessings. All members of the family make a point of attending this celebration and there may also be guests, Jewish or non-Jewish.

Special foods and wine are on the table. The youngest child asks his father four questions related to the observance of the Seder meal; the answers unfold the drama of the Exodus. The story is told as the foods are eaten. Unleavened matzoth recalls bread baked and eaten in flight; bitter herbs remind of slavery; a mixture of chopped nuts, apples, cinnamon, and wine represent mortar used in brickmaking; the dipping off of wine signifies sadness that Egypt had to suffer when Israel was freed. Blessings and songs of joy follow the Seder.

These and other ritual festivals remind the Jew of God's steadfast mercy on which he depends, remind him to repent and give thanks, and stress that God is served by acts of justice and kindliness. Arising in an agrarian society, the festivals continue to emphasize, even in an industrial community cut off from the soil, that man is called to respect God's purpose in creation and to enhance life—to engender, preserve, further, and perfect it. Particularly, this calling is stressed in family-centered rituals where members act out their remembering of what it means to be a Jew.

CHAPTER 5

Preparing to engage in dialogue

A PROGRAM

The preparation to engage in dialogue and suggestions for dialogue presented in this chapter are based on experiences of a program carried out in the Anglican Diocese of Toronto, Ontario. Material was prepared by Mrs. W. V. Rhodes under the direction of the Reverend Roland de Corneille, director of the program, and his assistant, Miss Phyllis Napier.

The program suggested may be used to prepare for dialogue with Jewish young people of your community. If you live in an area where there are few or no Jewish residents, the program may be followed by courses of study about Jewish faith and, perhaps, about the nature, causes, and dangers of prejudice.

Dialogue calls for an effort from us to state our own faith clearly, without compromise. So, we may need to strive for a deeper understanding of our own faith.

There is another, even harder, part to dialogue: we

must learn to listen—*really* listen—to the other person's expression of his faith and be willing to believe that he, too, is speaking from honest conviction. Through this speaking and listening we hope to understand more fully the faith of the other person and help him to understand our own faith more completely.

Dialogue, let us stress again, does not aim to convince the other person that he is wrong. Rather it aims to enable him and ourselves to examine the meaning of our different faiths and make responsible decisions of commitment. These decisions, together with our efforts and conversations, we offer up to God.

Dialogue, thus, must be a matter of deep conviction before it can be effective. When conviction exists, centuries-old walls of suspicion and prejudice can be broken down. This has been the experience of the work in the Diocese of Toronto. The old one-way street by which Christians reached Jews has given place to a two-way traffic in which ideas, hopes, and beliefs are shared.

As your group first decides to interest itself in dialogue between Christians and Jews, you may find that some members will mention Brotherhood Week as being an effort, already existing, to create better understanding between these groups. Happily it is true that, in many cities and towns, civic groups sponsor Brotherhood Week to bring together Christians and Jews who might not otherwise meet.

It is, however, the conviction of those engaged in the dialogue program that only direct and continuing Christian-Jewish involvement can allow for a thorough understanding of the problems that face each group in day-to-day living. Christians are well aware of the difficulties that face us as we try to apply Christian teachings at work, in school, in social life. The believing Jew is faced with equally great difficulties. In these areas Christians can speak openly and honestly with Jews about the problems and the ways in which we face them, and we can encourage Jews to do the same deep sharing with us.

The Program of Preparation

Five meetings of preparation preceded the program of Christian-Jewish Dialogue in the Diocese of Toronto. Some of them may not be possible for every group. The full program included:

First meeting | A look at our own attitudes
Second meeting | A review of past relationships between Jews and the Christian church
Third meeting | A tour of a synagogue
Fourth meeting | A discussion of how the church should be related to the Jew
Fifth meeting | The rules of dialogue

When your group decides it really wants to enter into dialogue with Jewish young people, discuss the idea thoroughly with your pastor. His training and knowledge will help you during some of the sessions. His leadership is important during this preparation for dialogue. He may know a rabbi or some Christian leader living nearby whose knowledge will also help you. In the Toronto Diocese lay leaders have been trained to assist in the program; you may be able to recruit similar leadership for your own group.

SESSION I—A LOOK AT OUR OWN ATTITUDES

The open-ended story is one method used in Toronto to introduce the preparation for dialogue to young people. Here is an example of a story that can help bring into the open the attitudes participants have toward Jews and some they have heard expressed:

The officers of a school entertainment club were being nominated. The school had a fairly large number of Jewish students in senior grades. One boy, Dave Grossman, was suggested by a member of the nominating committee to serve as treasurer.

"No can do," commented Bill Johnson. "He's a Jew."

Jay MacIntyre grinned. "Just the guy for the job."

"I don't see why we shouldn't have him," argued Sam Williams, the boy who had suggested Dave. "He's a good guy. Anyway, he's a whiz at math."

"All Jews are whizzes at math," said Bill. "It's all they are good at."

"That's not fair," Jay remarked angrily. "Dave is better at English than any of us."

"Besides, Dave's dad went bankrupt," threw in Bill. Jay looked thoughtful.

"That's right, too, a lot of Jews go bankrupt, don't they?"

Sam looked from one to the other. It was obvious that in a pinch Jay MacIntyre would vote with Bill Johnson. Yet Sam knew that Dave Grossman would be a fine treasurer with lots of ideas that would help the executive in other ways, too. Should he push ahead and formally nominate Dave and try to win over the others, or should he nominate someone else? All three boys were members of youth groups in their own churches. What should Sam Williams have done?

After the story has been read to the entire group, break into small groups, with leaders who can keep the discussion on the track, to talk over the attitudes shown in the story. What things that were said seemed true? Which seemed false? Why? What should Sam have done?

During the twenty to thirty minutes allowed for discussion, a recorder should note comments in each group. These should be reported to all when they meet at the end of the discussion period. Notes on the reports should be made on a blackboard so that points which constantly recur may be observed, giving a picture of the attitudes that do exist within the group.

In Toronto, comments reported from the small groups reflected their attitudes toward Jewish young people in their school. Comments showed that attitudes of parents and other members of the family played some part in the ways young people reacted to Jews. Not all found Jews to be congenial schoolmates. Accusations included that Jews were grasping, unethical, likely to cheat, and far too pampered at home. Jews were also said to avoid any form of manual work and to be reluctant to go out for sports. Girls expressed the opinion that Jewish girls are extravagant and overdressed.

The attitudes showed that even among young people who met Jews every day there was resentment and prejudice. Much of what they said was obviously repetition of things they had heard from adults. They had accepted, without thinking, the false stereotype of the Jew on which so much prejudice is based.

SESSION II—PAST RELATIONSHIPS BETWEEN THE JEWS AND THE CHURCH

This session may be led by your pastor. Its purpose is to explain the relationship between the Christian church and the Jews. No matter who presents this material, the following points may be used as guidelines:

1. Our Lord and all the first Christians were Jews; we understand the meaning of Jesus' life and death in terms of Old Testament concepts.

2. Christians are significantly responsible for the history of Jewish persecution of the past thousand years.

3. Our manner of praying, our hymns, other forms of worship, and some Christian architecture can be traced to Jewish origins. Check, for instance, how many hymns and prayers are derived from Jewish Worship.

An informal talk of not more than twenty or twenty-five minutes should be developed following these guidelines. Draw on material from this book and other resources indicated in the reading list on page 93. When the talk is finished, a question and answer period should follow. Some facts will probably come as a revelation to some members of the group. They should be given opportunity to ask whatever questions arise in their minds so they can get a clear picture of the facts.

SESSION III—TOUR OF A SYNAGOGUE

The pastor should have little difficulty in arranging such a tour. There is no doubt you will leave the synagogue with a great deal more information and with a better understanding than before.

The tour gives everybody an opportunity to see for themselves the interiors of the building they may see from the outside every day of their lives. They will see the magnificent scrolls of the Torah from which someone reads each Sabbath. They may be fortunate enough to meet with a group of Jewish young people who are eager to explain the meaning of the various symbols and to talk freely in the setting of the synagogue about the ceremonies of the Jewish faith.

SESSION IV—HOW THE CHURCH SHOULD BE RELATED TO THE JEW

This meeting takes the form of a discussion. The question for discussion is: What should our attitudes and relationship with the Jewish people be?

In discussing this, we should remind ourselves that

75

The interior of this contemporary synagogue displays ancient symbols, such as the burning bush, important to Jewish faith. The stained glass panel depicts the twelve tribes of Israel.

the gospel has a great deal to say about our relationships with all other persons. This, together with an understanding of our own attitudes toward Jews and some reasons for their attitudes toward us, can enable us to discuss what our attitudes toward Jewish neighbors should be.

Reporting sessions should follow small-group discussion of this question. Some prejudices may still exist, seemingly unaffected by all that has happened. More generally, however, an increased understanding of Jewish people will begin to emerge, along with a desire to know more about them.

In the Toronto program the preparation sessions have led young people to realize that each of us must put forth some effort to meet Jews more than half way. We must seek opportunities to know them and stop barricading ourselves behind walls of indifference.

Comments by some young people who have taken part in the programs run something like this:

"We are Christians and we do have a duty to love other people and to serve them."

"We should get to know them better."

"The gospel tells us to love our neighbors."

"We want to know more about the Jews."

"We should treat them just the same as we treat all the other people we know."

As the Toronto young people talk through their own responsibility as Christians, they realize their task is to love and serve and to witness as Christians in word and deed as well as in thought, and leave the results to God.

77

They come to the conclusion, even though they may phrase it in various ways, that what they need is dialogue between themselves as young Christian people and their young Jewish friends.

SESSION V—THE RULES OF DIALOGUE

The final step in the preparation is a session spent in careful study of the Rules of Dialogue written by Dr. Robert McAfee Brown (see Chapter 1). *This step may not be omitted.*

Copies of these rules should be given to each member of the group and there should be a sufficient number of copies for distribution among the Jewish group with whom they enter into dialogue. The rules should be read carefully and discussed thoroughly. No one should be allowed to take part in a dialogue unless he understands these rules and agrees to abide by them.

The minister is the best person to make arrangements for a dialogue between the young people and a Jewish young people's group. The rabbi and the minister can also decide the time and place for the first dialogue and its topic. Several young people from each group may be present to represent the interests and points of view of their groups. There is no limit to possible topics.

For example, in Toronto young people have discussed: "What are the difficulties for a teen-ager as a practicing Christian or Jew?" "Christian and Jewish prejudices—Why? Where?" "What do we believe is happening when we pray?" "What kind of influence does my faith have on the vocation I choose?"

Do not rush your planning. Prepare to meet in a place where small groups can separate to discuss topics without interfering with each other. Break into groups of eight or ten persons and assign leaders. Make sure you have a discussion leader for each group—which will, of course, be half Christian and half Jewish—and that everyone understands the topic under discussion. Plan to allow an hour or so for discussion and some time for reporting to the group as a whole afterward. At this time a recorder from each group can report briefly its views and discussion.

One arrangement that has proved successful is to have the Christian young people attend a Friday evening service at a synagogue, followed by the dialogue and light refreshments. Then on Sunday of the same weekend, have the Jewish young people attend a service at your church, followed by a dialogue and light refreshments. A tour of the church building could be offered so that the Jewish young people could learn even more about Christianity.

Of course, it is best to arrange for the food with the help of the rabbi so that there will be no conflict with dietary observances of the Jewish faith.

If you plan carefully, using imagination and good taste, you can have one of the most satisfying programs you have ever experienced.

Afterword

A dialogue between Rabbi Balfour Brickner and the Reverend David R. Hunter

Rabbi Brickner is Director of the Commission on Interfaith Activities for the Union of American Hebrew Congregations. Dr. Hunter is Deputy General Secretary of the National Council of the Churches of Christ in the U.S.A.

DR. HUNTER: What do you see to be the real value of a book like this?

RABBI BRICKNER: I think that the book has at least three values for me. First of all, it begins to fill in the blank pages that a lot of Christian young people have about Jewish life and Jewish religious values.

H: I agree. I think the average young Christian person is quite ignorant about Jews and Judaism. He knows something about the Jews from the Old Testament and he knows what he reads in the newspapers and he knows what he gets from community gossip.

B: There is certainly no knowledgeable relationship between his understanding of the Jew as the biblical personality and the Jew of the modern world. There is insufficient attempt made in Christian education to show how Rabbinic Judaism tied together the ancient and the modern. This book begins to show that relationship.

I find a second value in the book. It begins to commit Christianity to the responsibility of expiating its own sense of guilt for the shabby and sometimes cruel way it has treated Jews and Judaism in the past. As such this book is a first step in repentance.

H: That repentance is needed and I think this book at least begins to make that possible.

B: Thirdly, by having young people understand the roots of prejudice, as the book tries to do in some of its earlier chapters, it enables youth to deal more realistically with the things that make for prejudice. This is important even though I think that today's young people seem to be less prejudiced than their parents and grandparents.

H: I think this is probably true. Although I think that the young people are often the victims of certain pockets of anti-Semitism, from which they can't escape; they're just as adept at reflecting this as any adult is, if they live in the midst of it. If they have anti-Semitic parents, if they have neighbors who are caught up in some kind of extreme rightist movement that evidences anti-Semitic tendencies, young people can go to the same extremes as their elders. But I think your general statement is probably quite correct.

B: I find a problem with the book. The author expresses an ambivalence in regard to her understanding of the purpose of dialogue. Does dialogue mean just conversation or does it mean what she describes as the "parish approach," an attempt at conversion rather than conversation and understanding? This is not just her problem. Many Christians are ambivalent as they enter into dialogue. What is its purpose?

H: Her ambivalence is natural; it's common and I think it's inescapable. I think perhaps it ought to be inescapable. I think when we escape from the ambivalence that she demonstrates here, perhaps we're in a worse way as Christians trying to live in response to the Christian revelation.

B: Do you believe that the Christian attitude toward dialogue should be one of what she calls the "parish approach," seeking to win converts to Christendom?

H: I think my first answer to that would be no, not to convert. It's rather difficult to draw a line between the desire to convert and the desire to share with another person what one has that is of great value. But there is a difference between these two: it's a psychological difference with great human relations significance. Generally, people don't want to receive what someone else wants to force upon them, whether it's Christianity or something else. But the person who obviously values what he has and is ready to talk about it, without trying to push you into wanting to hear about it, is acting in an appropriate manner.

B: I can understand that. "Sharing," as you describe it, is part of the Christian mandate. Jews must come to understand that, without being offended by it. If Jews are still somewhat sensitive, cautious, even hostile to dialogue, it is because Christians have not always understood the word "dialogue" as you have put it.

H: And having been the victim of a conversion attempt, it's almost impossible to keep from interpreting the desire of a person to share as being essentially the same as seeking to convert.

B: Right. On page 22 in the Introduction, she says that "those who enter into dialogue with Jews must realize that Jews are committed to live as one people until God's Messiah ends time and brings in the new age." What does this mean? Does it mean that when this Messiah time comes, the Jews will cease being Jews? Will Christians cease to be Christian? Will the Messianic age be a Christian age or a Jewish age or a Buddhist age or a Muslim age?

H: I think all she means is that as a people you will no longer be precisely the people you were before.

B: But none of us will be.

H: True; I think that possibly that's all she means by it. I doubt if she means you will cease to be Jews and you will then be Christian.

B: Are you saying that when this Messianic age comes or comes again, we will all stop living as people with differences? We will all share common values in a common way? I'm not so sure I want the Messianic age under these conditions. For me the beauty of life is in its differences, not in its commonness; commonness often reduces itself to a lowest common denominator, to a mediocrity. I resist mediocrity and commonness.

H: The new age will be an age in which we all respond to God as we have not responded to him in the past. I'm not sure that the coming of the Messiah ends time. This is where I would perhaps quarrel with this writer. In fact, I don't think I'd ever conceived of time ending at the coming of the Messiah. But here she interprets the point of view of the Jews.

B: I must say that as I read through the second chapter, I was both delighted and troubled. I was delighted that Miss Althouse makes the flat assertion that Jews are not a race. They are not and it's good to hear somebody besides a Jew say it, for a change.

H: This is a very common misunderstanding.

B: But I was troubled by her effort to define the Jew in these terms alone. I wish I could say that the unique, distinctive, qualifying characteristic of what makes a Jew a Jew is his faith. But frankly I know many Jews, and so do you, who are atheists with no faith at all. They are still Jews.

She is right when she says a Jew is distinctly something more than just a child of certain parents. However, she is not correct when she says in the next sentence: "A Jew is one who believes he is one of a people chosen by God at Mt. Sinai." There are many Jews who have no understanding of chosenness and who are still Jews.

84

H: Just as there are plenty of Christians who have no understanding of their relationship to Christ.

B: It is not accurate to define a Jew exclusively in terms of chosenness.

    She makes the third element in the definition of a Jew in terms of rejection of the Trinity, the Triune I think she calls it. There is validity to this. But none of these define the Jew.

H: A Jew is a child of Jewish parents; but what else is he?

B: Well, he is a product of history. I think the one thing that you have to identify with the Jew is that he carries history with him, sometimes like a burden on his back and sometimes like a delightful gift. You cannot use the word Jew without being involved in a peculiar historical past, three, four thousand years, which is shared by elements of the Western world but which is to a large degree unique. He is motivated by history as nobody else.

    Chosenness and faithfulness and differences in understanding of divinity, one and unique as opposed to one with a uniqueness of three, are good distinctions but they should not be taken by anybody as exclusive distinctions.

H: They are part of his identity not always realized.

B: Correct, his identity is more than these. I was fascinated by the way in which she uses chosenness later on—where she refers to a quotation from 1 Peter.

H: ". . . you are a chosen race, a royal priesthood," page 40, in the second chapter.

B: In other words, this notion of chosenness is used in both Christendom and in Judaism; but chosenness in Christendom is different from chosenness in Judaism, at least as outlined here. In Christendom to be chosen is "to invite to fellowship." Whereas chosenness in Judaism, as she describes it, is "to live by example." Now is this a valid distinction for Christianity?

H: I don't think it's the whole truth about Christendom. I think it is correct that we are chosen to share the fellowship that we have in Jesus Christ with other people. I don't see mentioned in this same paragraph on page 40, however, the fact that we are chosen to share in Christ's mission in the world and this is a mission which is not basically a mission of conversion. It's a mission that has to do with God's active mission of love in the world.

B: That isn't what she says.

H: Actually that's omitted, I think.

B: She says, "We see that Christians are called to be something different from setting examples, though setting examples may be one way of fulfilling their task . . . invite all people to share their fellowship and way of life . . . to share redemption through Jesus Christ." Well, isn't this what we were talking about before—this idea of asking people to become Christian?

H: Well, I see a difference here between sharing and converting. And I'm glad she uses the word "share" here. It depends on whether you're going to push this fellowship that we enjoy down other people's throats, and that's the difference.

B: The one point that our conversation can highlight for the young people who read this book is that the idea of chosenness is present in both faiths. It is therefore ludicrous for anyone to condemn Jews or Judaism on the grounds that they see themselves or are seen as "a chosen people." First of all chosen has never meant being better than anyone else. Chosenness meant only great obligation and responsibility to both God and man, not something egotistical.

H: Actually I don't like the contrast that is set up in this paragraph. I'm not really satisfied with either of the explanations she gives. She says that Jews are chosen to set an example. If anybody asked me as a Christian whether this was correct I would say no, it is not the whole of it. I wonder if she is really doing justice to your concept of chosenness in that.

We are called at baptism into a ministry in the world. The sign of the cross is put on us at baptism to enter into that ministry which is not so much one of sharing, I would say, although that is a glorious aspect of it, as it is of doing, of joining with God in a ministry in life. This is a ministry of service, it's a ministry of reconciliation, and these have a substance to them that simply sharing does not have. While sharing is a part of it, I think simply to say that our chosenness is to be understood in terms of sharing is not to do justice to the depths of this ministry. And

I suspect that she isn't doing justice to the depths of your chosenness.

B: Yes, chosenness is more complex. It is to feel oneself under an obligation to God. It means that we are asked to take seriously this God who shepherds us through life and through history and to whom we feel a responsibility. Once you make that commitment, once you say "I choose God," certain things inevitably follow, certain things in terms of man-man relationships and certain things in terms of man-God relationships. When you reach this level, it seems to me that both Christianity and Judaism interpret the idea of chosenness in almost the same sort of way.

H: We have a degree of commonality there that I think needs much more exploration. God chose the Jews to enter into a covenant relationship that God established with his people.

B: This relationship implies that God needs man as much as man needs God. The more perfect society cannot be effected by God alone. Man is necessary.

H: Yes, I think that while I'm not sure he couldn't if he wanted to, he hasn't given any evidence of wanting to do it.

B: Yes, that's the point.

H: And I think that this adds a more substantial base to these two answers than I find in this paragraph.

B: In the second chapter Miss Althouse writes about Jewish nationalism. I would like to point out that the idea of return to Zion was not dependent upon the presence or absence of national rights at any given time or place.

H: Perhaps accelerated but not dependent.

B: Perhaps. When national rights were removed, intensification of the desire to return to Zion naturally grew. But Zionism, as it became known, was not merely a modern political development of Theodor Hertzl. It existed in the liturgy of the Jew for two thousand years; it was there as a sort of psychological prayer-wish. I must confess that there were times when Jews never really expected it would ever come about and it was Hertzl who gave it a modern impetus. But before there was Hertzl there was the cultural Zionist, Achad Haan, who wrote about the necessity to prepare oneself culturally and spiritually to merit return to Zion. Even in the period of the Golden Age in Spain, which was very much like the age in which we live today where Jews have full rights and great accessibility to the total community, a man like Jehuda Halevi wrote about the fulfillment of one's spiritual self in and through Zion, through Israel, Palestine.

H: If the Jews had been granted rights equal to the rights of others in all countries, however, do you suppose this longing for Zion, the creation of Zion, the return to Zion, would have been realized in this century?

B: Probably not. But the hope would have continued always. Unquestionably Hitler unwittingly speeded this process.

H: Rabbi Brickner, I would be interested in your reactions to the proposals made in this manuscript with reference to dialogue, the proposals encouraging dialogue.

B: I am heartened by the Christian encouragement of dialogue. Up to now most of this has come from the Jewish community. The warnings found in the fifth chapter, page 69, are ones that ought to be taken seriously. The experiences that I have had with dialogue have indicated to me that unless there is serious preparation prior to the entrance into dialogue, it will be a frustrating waste of time.

H: It's always important if one is entering into dialogue about anything to have some experience, direct experience in relation to what is going to be discussed. It just happens that in this area, our experience with the Jews, our experience actually has been very limited, has been haphazard. It certainly hasn't been identified and basically it hasn't been pursued.

B: Jews and Christians are often reluctant to go into a dialogue situation because they feel insecure in their knowledge of their own faith. Once they have had an opportunity to study, to feel secure about themselves as Jews and Christians, they can enter the dialogue with confidence. They, moreover, bring to the dialogue a useful wealth of knowledge.

H: Do you think then that the five point procedure in Chapter 5 is a fairly wise sequence?

B: Yes, I think it's an excellent sequence; this is the one that we also follow. I can certainly recommend it.

NOTES

Introduction

1. *The Church and the Jewish People,* a symposium edited by Göte Hedenquist and published by the International Missionary Council (London: Edinburgh House Press, 1954), see pp. 22-25 of the Introduction.
2. Findings of the Lutheran World Federation Consultation, "The Church and the Jewish People," *Lutheran World,* XI, No. 3, July, 1964, pp. 266, 267.
3. Gunther Harder, "Christian/Jewish Conversation," *Lutheran World,* XI, No. 3, July, 1964, p. 333.
4. *Ibid.,* p. 336.

Chapter 1

1. Robert L. Heilbroner, "Don't Let Stereotypes Warp Your Judgment," *Think,* June, 1961, reprinted with permission by the Anti-Defamation League of B'nai B'rith, New York.
2. *Ibid.*
3. From *An American Dialogue* by Robert McAfee Brown and Gustave Weigel. Copyright © 1960 by Robert McAfee Brown and Gustave Weigel. Reprinted by permission of Doubleday & Company, Inc.

Chapter 2

1. Lee A. Belford, *Introduction to Judaism,* an Association Press Reflection Book (New York: Association Press, 1961), p. 83.
2. Raphael H. Levine, *Two Paths to One God: Judaism and Christianity* (New York: Collier Books, 1962), p. 223.
3. Milton Steinberg, *Basic Judaism* (New York: Harcourt Brace and Company, 1947), p. 59.
4. Ben Zion Bokser, *Judaism: Profile of a Faith* (New York: Alfred A. Knopf, 1963), p. 161.

5. Harry Emerson Fosdick, *Great Voices of the Reformation* (New York: The Modern Library, Random House, Inc., 1952), p. 180.
6. *Union Prayerbook,* I, Revised Edition, p. 34.

Chapter 3

1. Belford, *op. cit.,* p. 62.
2. "Conservative Judaism," *Meet the American Jew,* edited by Belden Menkus with the assistance of Rabbi Arthur Gilbert (Nashville: Broadman Press, 1963), p. 53.

Chapter 4

1. Joshua Fishman, *The Jewish Family* (New York: Anti-Defamation League of B'nai B'rith), p. 13.
2. Arthur Gilbert and Oscar Tarcov, *Your Neighbor Celebrates* (New York: B'nai B'rith Anti-Defamation League), p. 9.
3. Levine, *op. cit.,* p. 79.
4. Gilbert and Tarcov, *op. cit.,* p. 17.

READING LIST

To learn more about Jews and Judaism, consider reading and using:

American Jews: Their Story, by Oscar Handlin. New York: B'nai B'rith Anti-Defamation League (515 Madison Ave., New York, N. Y., 10022). 35 cents.

Basic Judaism, by Milton Steinberg. New York: Harcourt Brace and Co., 1947. $2.50.

Judaism and Prayer, "Issues of Faith" series, by Rabbi Herbert M. Baumgard. New York: Union of American Hebrew Congregations, 1964. Hard cover, $1.50.

Judaism: Profile of a Faith, by Ben Zion Bokser. New York: Alfred A. Knopf, 1963. $5.00.

Kit of Religious Articles. Contains (some in miniature) religious and ceremonial items used in Jewish worship; copies of the *Passover Haggadah, The Sabbath, Your Neighbor Worships, Your Neighbor Celebrates,* and a comprehensive illustrated guide for instruction. Available on loan or for purchase from the Anti-Defamation League. Purchase, $10.00.

The Church and the Jewish People, edited by Göte Hedenquist. London: Edinburgh House Press, 1954.

The Church and the Jews, a study handbook by Göte Hedenquist. London: Edinburgh House Press, 1961. Available from World Council of Churches, Room 440, 475 Riverside Drive, New York, N. Y., 10027. 35 cents.

When Faith Meets Faith, by David M. Stowe. New York: Friendship Press, 1963. Paper, $1.95.

Your Neighbor Celebrates, by Rabbi Arthur Gilbert and Oscar Tarcov, New York: B'nai B'rith Anti-Defamation League. Hard cover, $2.50; paper, 35 cents.

Your Neighbor Worships, by Rabbi Arthur Gilbert. New York: B'nai B'rith Anti-Defamation League. Paper, 25 cents.

To get the facts about prejudice, and especially about anti-Semitism, read these:

ABC's of Scapegoating, by Gordon Allport. 40-page Anti-Defamation League (ADL) pamphlet, 35 cents.

Anti-Semitism in America, by Melvin M. Tumin. 16-page ADL pamphlet, 25 cents.

Danger in Discord, by Oscar and Mary F. Handlin. 32-page ADL pamphlet, 50 cents.

Faith and Prejudice, by Bernhard E. Olson. New Haven and London: Yale University Press, 1962. $7.50.

Prejudice and Society, by Earl Raab and Seymour M. Lipset. 40-page ADL pamphlet, 35 cents.

Sense and Nonsense About Race, by Ethel J. Alpenfels. New York: Friendship Press, 1965 (second revision). 75 cents.

Small-Town Jews and Their Neighbors in the United States, by Peter I. Rose. ADL reprint, 25 cents.

Social Discrimination Against Jews in America, 1830-1930, by John Higham. ADL reprint, 40 cents.

To become familiar with dialogue programs, read these:

"Come Let Us Reason Together," A Guide for Establishing Lay Dialogue in Congregational Interreligious Activity, introduction by Rabbi Balfour Brickner. New York: The Commission on Interfaith Activities, a joint commission of the Union of American Hebrew Congregations (838 Fifth Ave., New York, N. Y.) Free. *(Reform)*

An Interfaith Weekend Conclave for Youth, introduction by Rabbi Balfour Brickner. New York: The Commission on Interfaith Activities. 50 cents.

CREDITS

The sources for the photographs in this book appear below.

ABOUT THE FORMAT

TYPE: Times Roman 11 pointed leaded 2 points

COMPOSITION, PRESS, AND BINDING: Sowers Printing Company,
    Lebanon, Pennsylvania

PAPER COVERS: Affiliated Lithographers, Inc., New York

TEXT PAPER: Crestopake Text Vellum Finish

TYPOGRAPHIC DESIGN: Margery W. Smith